Guess What!

Student's Book 5

American English

Susannah Reed with **Kay Bentley**
Series Editor: Lesley Koustaff

CAMBRIDGE
UNIVERSITY PRESS

Contents

Around the world

1 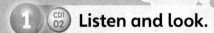 Listen and look.

2  Listen and repeat. Then match.

①

②

③

④

⑤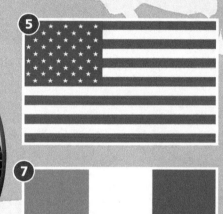

⑥

⑦

⑧

⑨

⑩

> **a** Brazil **b** China **c** Colombia **d** France **e** Italy **f** Mexico
> **g** Russia **h** Spain **i** the United Kingdom **j** the United States

3 Listen and answer the questions. Then practice with a friend.

> Which country has a yellow, blue, and red flag? Colombia!

4 Which countries do you want to visit? Ask and answer.

5 CD1 05 **Read and listen.**

Jules and Denis: We're from France.

Rosa: I'm from the United States, but my father's from Spain.

Maria: I'm from Brazil.

Anton: I'm from Russia.

Focus!
Where are you from?
I'm from the United States.
Is he from France?
Yes, he is.
No, he isn't.

6 **Match the questions and answers. Then ask and answer.**

1 Where is Rosa from?
2 Where are Jules and Denis from?
3 Is Maria from Brazil?
4 Is Anton from Italy?
5 Where is Rosa's father from?

a He's from Spain.
b No, he isn't. He's from Russia.
c They're from France.
d She's from the United States.
e Yes, she is.

7 My World **Answer the questions. Then ask a friend.**

Where are you from?
Where are your friends from?

Where are your parents from?
Where are your grandparents from?

8 CD1 06 **Go to page 102. Listen and repeat the chant.**

→ Workbook page 5

9 When is Carla's birthday? Listen and choose.

a in February   b in April   c in August

 10 Listen again and practice.

Alex: When's your birthday, Carla?
Carla: On April 24th.
Alex: So is mine! When were you born?
Carla: I was born in 2006. On April 24th, 2006.
Alex: Oh! I was born in 2006, too!
Carla: Where were you born?
Alex: I was born in the United Kingdom. What about you?
Carla: I was born in Spain.

Focus!

1st, 2nd, 3rd, 4th, 5th, 6th, 7th, 8th, 9th, 10th
When were you born?
I was born on April 24th, 2006.

 11 Read about the children. Then ask and answer.

Emma
Date of birth:
June 2nd, 2005
Place of birth:
the United States

Alex
Date of birth:
April 24th, 2006
Place of birth:
the United Kingdom

Carla
Date of birth:
April 24th, 2006
Place of birth:
Spain

Pedro
Date of birth:
January 31st, 2005
Place of birth:
Brazil

When was Alex born?   On April 24th, 2006.

Where was he born?   He was born in the United Kingdom.

Say it!

 12 How many syllables are there in each word? Listen, count, and repeat.

Spain   **birth**-day   Oc-**to**-ber

13 (CD1 10) **Read and listen.**

1 WORLD QUIZ — How many questions can you answer? A PRIZE FOR THE WINNERS!

It sounds fun! Let's take the quiz together!

Hey, Ruby, look at this!

2 What's the first question, Jack?

Which city in Colombia has a flower festival?

3 My pen pal, Sofia, is from Colombia! We can email her.

OK, let's go to the reading room.

4 Where is everyone?

This isn't the reading room!

5 Listen to this!

To win the quiz,
Let's play a game.
Answer the questions,
And come home again.

START

6 What should we do?

Let's play the game. We want to win the quiz!

7 What's happening?

8

Value: Try new things   **9**

Skills: *Listening and speaking*

 What do people do at festivals?

14 **Where are these festivals? Listen and match.**

a Brazil   **b** China   **c** Spain   **d** the United Kingdom   **e** the United States

1

Bonfire Night, Lewes

2

Feria, Seville

3

New Year, Shanghai

4

Carnival, Rio de Janeiro

5

Independence Day, New York

15 **Listen again and say the missing words.**
1 Bonfire Night is on   5th.
2 Feria is always in   .
3 Chinese New Year is in   or   .
4 The Carnival in Rio de Janeiro starts on a   .
5 Independence Day is on   4th.

16   **Plan a tour of some festivals.**

Which festivals would you like to go to?   I'd like to go to …

Where are they?   The … is in …

Skills: *Reading and writing*

Look below! **What does Kiara want to be?**

17 (CD1 13) **Read and listen.**

Kiara is eleven years old, and she's from Moscow in Russia. Kiara wants to be a dancer. She goes to dance classes every week. She wants to dance at the Russian Winter Festival.

The Russian Winter Festival takes place every year in Moscow, in December and January.

Moscow is very cold in the winter, and there's a lot of snow. There are a lot of fun activities at the festival. You can go on a troika ride through the snow. Or you can go ice-skating in the city. There are also lots of beautiful snow sculptures.

At night, you can watch the fireworks. Or you can go and see a show with traditional singers and dancers. Look out for Kiara!

18 **Read again and correct the sentences.**
1 Moscow is in China.
2 Kiara wants to be an artist.
3 The Winter Festival is in November and January.
4 It's hot in the winter in Russia.
5 You can go swimming in the city.
6 You can watch fireworks in the morning.

Moscow isn't in China. It's in Russia.

Your turn! **Think of a festival you enjoy.**
When is it?
Which country is it in?
What can you see there?
What can you do there?

Now write about it in your notebook.

What are mosaics made of?

1 CD1 14 Listen and repeat.

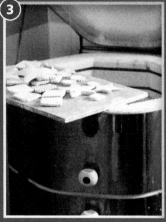

tiles   marble   ceramic   glue

2 Watch the video.

3 CD1 15 Read and listen.

There are lots of different mosaics in countries around the world. Mosaics are made of many small tiles. These tiles are different shapes and colors, and are made of ceramic, glass, paper, or stones, like marble.

Artists put glue on mosaic tiles and then make pictures or patterns with them. Sometimes artists glue the tiles onto cardboard first, then stick the cardboard with the mosaics onto walls, floors, and roofs.

In the past, mosaics in Roman gardens and baths were made of round stones or shells. Today, artists make mosaics for places like train stations and shopping malls to make them look beautiful.

Guess What!

In Spain, some artists used spoons, forks, and knives in mosaics.

Project

6 Find out about a mosaic in your country. Make a fact file about it.

Artist: Antoni Gaudi
Place: Park Güell in Barcelona, Spain

It's made of lots of colored tiles. The tiles are made of glass and stone. It's very beautiful.

4 Answer the questions.

1 What kind of art has many small tiles?
2 What can the tiles be made of?
3 Where were there very old mosaic floors?
4 Why do artists make mosaics today?

5 Where would you put a mosaic in your school?

1 Family and pets

Guess What!

1 (CD1 16) **Listen and look.**

2 (CD1 17) **Listen and repeat. Then match.**

1 my grandparents

2 my aunt

3 my parents

4 my uncle

5 my sister

6 my brother

7 my cousin

8 my best friend

9 my kitten

10 my puppy

a artistic   b smart   c friendly   d funny   e hardworking
f kind   g naughty   h shy   i sporty   j talkative

3 (CD1 18) (Think) **Listen and guess who. Then practice with a friend.**

They're friendly.   They're Alex's grandparents!

4 (My World) **What is your family like? Ask and answer.**

5 **Read and listen.**

Focus!

My dog is smarter than my cat.
My brother is more hardworking than my sister.

I'm more talkative than
my cousin,
She's shyer than me.
And I'm friendlier than
my cousin,
But she's kinder than me.

6 **Listen and choose the words.**

I'm **more artistic/more hardworking** than my brother,
He's **funnier/sportier** than me.
And I'm **more hardworking/more talkative** than my brother,
But he's **smarter/kinder** than me.

7 **Make questions. Then ask a friend.**

Are you	more talkative	than your sister?
Is your brother	friendlier	than you?
Is your sister	more hardworking	than your brother?
Is your cousin	smarter	than your cousin?
Is your friend	more artistic	than your friend?

Are you friendlier than your sister?

Yes, I am!

8 **Go to page 102. Listen and repeat the chant.**

What are they talking about? Listen and choose.
a friends   b height   c age

 Listen again and practice.
Teacher: Who's taller, Carla – you or Emma?
Emma: I am!
Carla: Hmm. Let's see … I am!
Teacher: Wow! You're taller than Emma now!
Emma: But I'm still older than you, Carla!
Teacher: And who's smarter?
Carla: Oh, I don't know. We're both smart!

Focus!
Who's older,
you or your brother?
My brother is.

11 **Read about Emma and Alex. Then ask and answer.**

Name: Emma
Born: June 2nd, 2005
Height: 1 m, 60 cm
Personality: quiet, but friendly
Likes: sports and homework

Name: Alex
Born: April 24th, 2006
Height: 1 m, 52 cm
Personality: loud and funny
Likes: art and talking to my friends

artistic   funny   hardworking   old   quiet
short   sporty   talkative   tall   young

Who is older?

Emma is!

Say it!

 Which syllables sound the strongest? Listen and repeat.

pup-py   re-**peat**   **talk**-a-tive   hard-**work**-ing

13 🎧 CD1 25 **Read and listen.**

1 Which city in Colombia has a flower festival?

Wow! I think we're at the flower festival.

And look at this! It's a message!

I can help you with your game! My friend Ruby knows my name. Look for me in the parade. I'm taller than both of you today.

2 Hmm, I think it's from Sofia. She's very smart, but she isn't taller than us.

3 Look, Ruby!

It's Sofia!

4 Hi Sofia! Can you help us?

Of course.

We're taking a quiz.

5 The first question is about the flower festival.

Yes … ?

Where are we?

6 Guess!

MEDELLIN

Of course! We're in Medellín.

7 We're moving again.

Come with us, Sofia.

Where to?

→ Workbook page 15

Value: Learn about other cultures 19

Skills: *Listening and speaking*

Let's start! What can you see at a circus?

14 (CD1 26) What's life like in a circus family?
Listen and say the letters.

a

Show time in the circus.

b

Sonia at home.

c

The circus at night.

d

Circus life is hard work!

15 (CD1 26) **Listen again and say *true* or *false*.**

1 Sonia's twelve years old.
2 Sonia's older than her brothers and sisters.
3 Sonia's family is hardworking.
4 Sonia's grandparents are clowns.
5 Sonia doesn't go to school.

16 (CD1 27) (Talk Time) **Ask about a friend's family.**

What's your cousin like?   He's/She's ...

What are your parents like?   They're ...

Skills: *Reading and writing*

 What are these children good at?

17 **Read and listen.**

Hot shots

Brad Miller and his older sister, Casey, are from the United States. Brad is eleven, and Casey is thirteen. They're both sporty, and they're both very good at playing basketball.

Brad and Casey play on basketball teams. The other players on their teams are older and taller than them, but Brad and Casey are the star players. They practice basketball every day. Someday they want to play for the Los Angeles Lakers.

Smart artists

Abby and Bianca Watson are twins. They're twelve years old, and they're from the United Kingdom. They're very good at art, and they like painting with bright colors. The twins sell their paintings in stores and art galleries.

This painting is by Abby. It's called "Nature."

18 **Read again and answer the questions.**
1. Where are Brad and Casey from?
2. Who is older, Brad or Casey?
3. Are Brad and Casey hardworking?
4. Are Abby and Bianca from France?
5. Is Bianca older than Abby?
6. Where do they sell their paintings?

Your turn!

Think of someone you know.
How old are they?
What are they good at?
What do they work hard at?

Now write about it in your notebook.

→ Workbook page 17

How do
ant families
work
together?

1 CD1 29 Listen and repeat.

worker ant · colony · queen ant · drone · nest

2 Watch the video.

3 CD1 30 Read and listen.

Ants live in families called colonies. In each colony, ants work together in groups and help one another. Most colonies of ants live in nests, and every colony has one queen ant. The queen's job is to make lots and lots of eggs for the colony.

There are also drone ants and worker ants in colonies. The drones help the queen to make eggs, and the worker ants do all of the other jobs. There are always lots of worker ants. Some of them make the nest and keep it neat and clean. Other worker ants find food, like leaves, and bring it back to the nest.

Guess What!

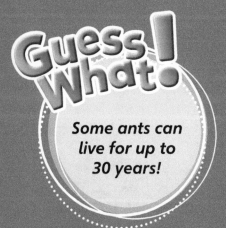

Some ants can live for up to 30 years!

Project

6 Find out about animal families in your country. Make a story poster and show how the animal family works together.

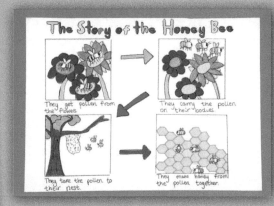

4 Answer the questions.

1 What are ant families called?
2 What does the queen ant do?
3 What do the drone ants do?
4 What do the worker ants do?

5 What do you like about working in a group?

On the playground

Guess What!

1 ^{CD1 31} **Listen and look.**

2 ^{CD1 32} **Listen and repeat. Then match.**

a cry   b litter   c help others   d hop   e shout
f skip   g laugh   h text a friend   i throw a ball   j use a cell phone

3 ^{CD1 33} **Listen and say the numbers. Then practice with a friend.**

They're skipping.   Number 2!

4 My World **What do you do in school? Ask and answer.**

5 **Read and listen.**

Our school rules

✓
- We should be hardworking and listen to the teachers.
- We should be polite and help people.
- We should put litter in the trash cans.

✗
- We shouldn't shout in class.
- We shouldn't be naughty or laugh at people.
- We shouldn't litter on the ground.

 6 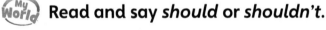 **Read and say *should* or *shouldn't*.**

1 We _____ do our homework.
2 We _____ eat and drink in the classroom.
3 We _____ use cell phones in school.
4 We _____ wash our hands before lunch.
5 We _____ listen to music in the classroom.
6 We _____ be quiet in the library.

Focus!

We **should** be polite and help people.
We **shouldn't** shout in class.

7 **Make school rules with a friend.**

We should play nicely with our friends. We shouldn't run in the classroom.

 8 **Go to page 102. Listen and repeat the chant.**

What does Alex have in school? Listen and choose.

a a computer game b a cell phone c a pencil case

 Listen again and practice.

Teacher:	OK, Pedro. Read us the story, please.
Alex:	Uh-oh!
Teacher:	Alex! Do you have a cell phone?
Alex:	Yes, I do.
Teacher:	You shouldn't use cell phones in school. Bring me the phone, please.
Alex:	Here you are. I'm sorry.
Teacher:	OK, now …
Pedro:	Uh-oh!

Focus!

Bring me the phone, please.
Tell the class about your vacation, please.

11 (Think) **Read and match. Then give instructions to your friend.**

1 Give Anna your book, please.

2 Bring me the ball, please.

3 Tell the class about your vacation, please.

4 Pass Max a ruler, please.

Bring me the ball, please.   Here you are.

Say it!

12 **Which words sound the strongest? Listen and repeat.**

Give Anna your **book.**   **Pass Max** a **ruler.**

13 CD1 39 **Read and listen.**

1 Where are capuchin monkeys from?

Where are we?

We're in a market.

It's London in 1850.

2 Look at this poor monkey. His name's Capu.

Let's give him some fruit.

3 Stop! You shouldn't feed my monkey.

Uh-oh! Run!

4 Let's hide in here.

I think it's a school.

5 Phew!

6 We're in a classroom!

And look! It's the monkey!

7 He's from South America. He's a capuchin monkey.

He wants to go home!

8 We can take Capu!

Yes, but we have to be quick!

→ Workbook page 23

Value: Be kind to animals   29

Skills: *Listening and speaking*

Let's start! What games do you like playing on your playground?

14 (CD1 40) How do you play *Queenie, Queenie*? Listen and say the letters.

15 (CD1 40) Put the rules in order. Listen again and check.

a You need more than two players.

b The Queenie throws the ball behind her. She doesn't look.

c The Queenie guesses who has the ball.

d One player is the Queenie. She takes the ball and turns around.

e Another player catches the ball.

16 (CD1 41) **Talk Time** Invent or describe a game.

You need ... players.

You ...

One player ...

Another player ...

Skills: *Reading and writing*

(Look below!) **Where are these schools?**

17 (CD1 42) **Read and listen. Then match.**

Kanta is from Bangladesh. Sometimes it is very rainy, and the children can't go to school. So a school boat comes to Kanta's village. The boat has a classroom and a small library with computers. Students study hard. Kanta studies for three hours every day. She learns math, reading, writing, English, and Bengali.

a

Alfie is from the United Kingdom. He loves reading, and he often goes to the library at his school. The library is in a bus on the playground! The bus has two floors, and there are lots of books. Students can also go to the library before and after school with their parents.

b

18 **Read again and say *true*, *false*, or *don't know*.**

1 Kanta goes to school on a boat.
2 Alfie studies for three hours a day.
3 There isn't a library in Kanta's school boat.
4 Alfie loves reading.
5 There are computers in Alfie's library.
6 Kanta studies every day.

Your turn!
Design an unusual school.
Where is it: on a boat, in a plane, in a treehouse?
What subjects do the students study?
What rules should they follow?

Now write about it in your notebook.

Where are the places on the map?

Central Park East School

Hudson River

Metropolitan Museum

Central Park Zoo

Time Warner Center

N
W E
S

1 (CD1 43) **Listen and repeat.**

1 north

5 compass

4 west

2 east

3 south

2 **Watch the video.**

3 (CD1 44) **Read and listen.**

A compass helps us find places on a map. This map of New York Central Park shows what is in and close to the park.

To the southwest of the park, we can see a big shopping mall, and we can see a zoo in the southeast. To the west of the park, there is the Hudson River. It runs from the north to the south of New York State. In the east of the park, we can see a famous museum with art from around the world. To the northeast of the park, there's a school.

This map has a compass. It shows N, E, S, and W. It's easy to find places you want to visit.

Guess What!

The very first maps showed the stars, not our world!

Project

6 **Find out about places close to your school.**
Draw a map with the places and a compass on it.

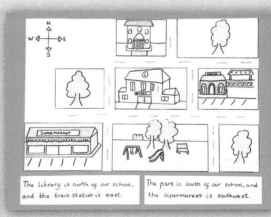

The library is north of our school, and the train station is east.

The park is south of our school, and the supermarket is southwest.

4 **Answer the questions.**

1 What's to the southwest of the park?
2 Where's the Hudson River on the map?
3 Where's the school on the map?
4 What do N, E, S, and W mean?

5 **When do you use a map with a compass?**

CLIL: Geography **33**

Review Units 1 and 2

1 Read, listen, and choose the words.

This is my pen pal, Lola. She's from **Brazil/Mexico**. We're both **eleven/twelve**, but she's **older/younger** than me. She was born on October **2nd/4th**, and I was born on October **22nd/24th**.

Lola and I are both **sporty/artistic**, and we love **painting/soccer**. I think she's a little **smarter/kinder** than me, though.

Lola writes to me every month, and she sends me photographs – like this one. Sometimes we **phone/text** each other. Lola is very **funny/shy**, and her letters always make me **laugh/smile**.

Lola says I **should/shouldn't** visit her one day. I'd love to!

Nadia

2 Read again and correct the sentences.
1 Nadia is eleven years old.
2 Lola was born on November fourth.
3 Nadia is older than Lola.
4 Lola sends Nadia paintings.
5 Lola isn't very funny.

3 Think of a friend or pen pal. Ask and answer.

Where's he/she from?
When was he/she born?
What's he/she like?

4 Write about your friend or pen pal in your notebook.

34

→ Workbook page 28

5 Play the game.

17
You ▓▓▓ work hard in school.

18
born? / friend / was / your / When

19
GO BACK TWO SQUARES!

20
GOOD JOB!

16
GO FORWARD ONE SQUARE!

15
A ▓▓▓ person likes running, hopping, and skipping!

14
aunt / Mexico? / from / your / Is

13
You shouldn't ▓▓▓ at other people.

9
A ▓▓▓ person talks a lot.

10
THROW AGAIN!

11
You shouldn't ▓▓▓ cell phones in school.

12
artistic / parents / you? / more / than / Are / your

8
homework? / always / you / do / your / Do

7
START AGAIN!

6
father / the / States? / your / Is / from / United

5
You shouldn't ▓▓▓ on the playground.

1
START

2
born / Russia? / Were / in / you

3
A ▓▓▓ person often helps other people.

4
shyer, / you / your / Who / is / or / friend ?

Blue
Make a question.

Orange
Say the missing words.

3 Under the ocean

Guess What!

1 (CD2 02) **Listen and look.**

2 (CD2 03) **Listen and repeat. Then match.**

a crab   b dolphin   c jellyfish   d octopus   e seal
f shark   g starfish   h stingray   i turtle   j whale

3 (CD2 04) (Think) **Listen and guess the animals. Then practice with a friend.**

It has gray fur. It's smaller than a dolphin.   It's a seal!

4 (My World) **What's your favorite sea animal? Ask and answer.**

5 CD2 05 **Read and listen.**

Dolphins are the most intelligent sea animals. They are the friendliest, too.

Blue whales are the biggest sea animals. They are the heaviest and the strongest, too.

Great white sharks are the most dangerous sharks, but they aren't the most dangerous sea animals.

Box jellyfish are the most dangerous sea animals.

Focus!

the strong**est**
the heav**iest**
the most dangerous

6 **Read and say *true* or *false*.**

1 Blue whales are the weakest sea animals.

2 Dolphins are the most dangerous sea animals.

3 Great white sharks are the most dangerous sharks.

4 Box jellyfish are the friendliest sea animals.

7 My World **Make sentences about sea animals. Then talk to a friend.**

Turtles are the most beautiful sea animals.

Yes, I agree.

No, I don't agree. I think dolphins are the most beautiful.

Say it!

8 CD2 06 CD2 07 **Which syllables sound the strongest? Listen and repeat.**

Jellyfish are **dan**gerous.   **Dol**phins are in**tell**igent.

What are they talking about? Listen and choose.

a land animals   b birds   c sea animals

 Listen again and practice.

Carla: Hi, Alex. What are you doing?

Alex: I'm taking a quiz about animals.

Carla: Can I help?

Alex: OK. Question one. Which sea animal is the fastest? Is it a turtle, a dolphin, or a seal?

Carla: Hmm. I think it's a dolphin. Yes. A dolphin.

Alex: Yes! Good job!

Carla: OK. Question two …

Focus!

Which sea animal is the fastest?
It's a dolphin.

  Look at the quiz. Make questions and ask and answer. Then listen and check.

Which fish is the heaviest?   It's a whale shark.

Are you an animal whiz? Try our animal quiz.

1 fish/heavy?
a) blue shark
b) whale shark
c) great white shark

2 bird/strong?
a) eagle
b) penguin
c) owl

3 land animal/strong?
a) gorilla
b) elephant
c) bear

4 land animal/tall?
a) kangaroo
b) panda
c) giraffe

5 sea animal/slow?
a) crab
b) seahorse
c) starfish

6 land animal/dangerous?
a) hippo
b) lion
c) tiger

 Go to page 102. Listen and repeat the chant.

13 CD2 11 **Read and listen.**

1 What is a dolphin family called?

What? My feet are wet!

Where are we now?

Let's see.

2 We're in Africa.

I think this is the Indian Ocean.

It's beautiful.

3 What's that? Is it trash?

I don't know.

4 Look! It's a baby dolphin.

Poor thing!

5 Quick! Help me find some shells.

Capu has the biggest shell.

6 Cut it like this …

Be careful, Jack!

7 Look! It's the dolphin's pod.

They're very friendly.

→ Workbook page 33

8 They're saying thank you!

It was a pleasure!

Value: Keep our seas and oceans clean

41

Skills: *Listening and speaking*

Let's start! What can you see at an aquarium?

14 Which animals do they see? Listen and say the letters.

a

See our baby dolphins.

b

Touch a stingray.

c

Feed our friendly seals.

d

Meet Otto.

e

Get close to our sharks.

15 CD2 12 Listen again and say the missing words.

1 Otto is the _____ octopus in the world.
2 Ava and Paco see _____ baby dolphins.
3 Ava thinks _____ are dangerous.
4 The time is _____ .
5 They can feed the _____ at a quarter after three.

16 CD2 13 (Talk Time) Plan a trip for this weekend.

Where would you like to go this weekend?

I'd like to go to …

How can you get there?

You can go by …

Skills: *Reading and writing*

 Look below! **What does the Sea Turtle Rescue Center do?**

17 **Read and listen.**

Save Our Sea Turtles

Turtles are one of the most beautiful animals in the ocean, but they are also in danger. How can we help them?

We should keep our oceans clean. Turtles eat jellyfish, crabs, other sea animals, and plants. Dirty oceans are dangerous to turtles and the food they eat.

We should protect turtle nests. Turtles lay their eggs in nests on the beach. Sometimes birds and other animals eat the eggs or baby turtles.

Sea Turtle Rescue Center

The Sea Turtle Rescue Center has safe beaches for turtles and their nests. It helps sick turtles in its animal hospital. Then it puts the healthy turtles back into the ocean. Turtles are happiest in the ocean.

18 **Read again and answer the questions.**
1 Are turtles dangerous?
2 How can we help turtles?
3 What do turtles eat?
4 Where do turtles lay their eggs?
5 What does the Sea Turtle Rescue Center do?
6 Where are turtles happiest?

 Your turn!

Think of a sea animal.
Where does it live?
What does it eat?
Is it in danger?

Now write about it in your notebook.

→ Workbook page 35

What is an **underwater food chain?**

1 CD2 15 **Listen and repeat.**

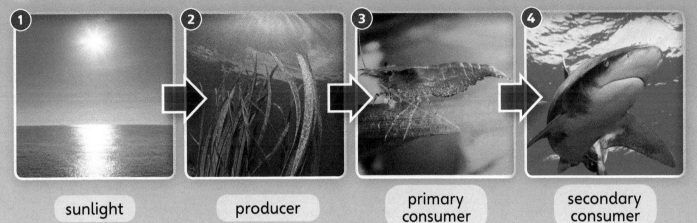

sunlight   producer   primary consumer   secondary consumer

2 **Watch the video.**

3 CD2 16 **Read and listen.**

Many plants and animals live underwater. How does an underwater food chain work? It needs sunlight, producers, primary consumers, and secondary consumers.

Sunlight shines on the ocean, and some sunlight goes under the water. Plants use the sunlight to make, or produce, food inside their leaves. We call these plants "producers."

Fish and other sea animals can't make their own food. They need to eat, or consume, plants and other fish. Some small sea animals or fish eat underwater plants. We call these fish "primary consumers."

Then bigger sea animals or fish, like stingray, eat smaller fish and other sea animals. They are called "secondary consumers." Big secondary consumers like sharks eat animals like seals!

Guess What!

Great white sharks can live for up to three months without food.

Project

6 **Find out about another food chain. Draw a picture and write about it.**

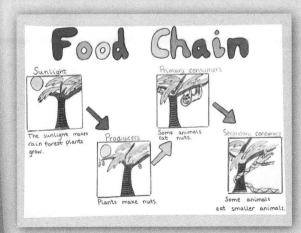

4 **Answer the questions.**

1 What helps plants make food inside their leaves?
2 Are producers plants or animals?
3 What do we call fish that eat plants?
4 What do secondary consumers eat?

5 **Which other food chains can you describe?**

→ Workbook page 36

4 Gadgets

Guess What!

47

1 (CD2 17) **Listen and look.**

2 (CD2 18) **Listen and repeat. Then match.**

a digital camera   **b** e-reader   **c** games console   **d** headphones   **e** laptop
f MP4 player   **g** smartphone   **h** tablet   **i** television   **j** video camera

3 (CD2 19) (Think) **Listen and answer the questions. Then practice with a friend.**

Can you listen to music on an MP4 player?   Yes, you can!

4 (My World) **What gadgets do you have? Ask and answer.**

5 (CD2 20) **Read and listen.**

Luisa: I listened to music on an MP4 player in a watch!

Tia: I didn't play games or watch a movie. I studied English on an e-reader.

Max and Adam: We didn't listen to music. We played great games on the consoles.

Lottie and Simon: We watched a movie on a tablet. We used some cool headphones.

6 **Read and say the names.**

1 They played on the games consoles.
2 She didn't watch a movie.
3 She used an e-reader.
4 She listened to music on an MP4 player.
5 They didn't play on the games consoles. They watched a movie.

Focus!

I studied English.
I listened to music on an MP4 player.
We didn't listen to music.

7 (My World) **Make true and false sentences about you. Then talk to a friend.**

listened to	a games console	yesterday evening
watched	my MP4 player	last night
played on	television	last Saturday
used	my laptop	this morning before school

I watched television this morning before school.   False.

8 (CD2 21) **Go to page 102. Listen and repeat the chant.**

9 Who did Emma visit last weekend? Listen and choose.

a her cousins   b her friends   c her grandparents

 10 Listen again and practice.

Carla: Hi, Emma. What did you do last weekend?
Emma: I visited my grandparents.
Carla: Was it fun?
Emma: Yes, it was great.
Carla: What did you do?
Emma: We watched television, and we played on their new games console.
Carla: Do your grandparents have a games console?
Emma: Yes, they do. They love playing games!

 11 **My World** Choose four activities you did last weekend. Then talk to some friends.

> **Focus!**
>
> What did you do last weekend?
> I visited my grandparents.

What did you do last weekend?   I played soccer.

So did I.   I didn't. I visited my cousins.

listened to music | played with friends | played soccer | called a friend | used a laptop

played on a games console | watched television | walked in the park | cleaned my room | painted a picture

helped my parents | studied English

Say it!

 12 Can you hear the different endings? Listen and repeat.

/d/	/t/	/id/
played	watched	visited

13 🎧 CD2 25 Read and listen.

1

Do trees grow in Antarctica?

It's cold.

There's nothing here!

Only snow! Let's go in that hut.

2

I think we're in Antarctica.

It's 1950. Look at this diary.

3

Listen to this!

...rrived this ...ning. The hut ...ery cold, and ...don't have any ...ood.

4

Where are they now?

What is it, Capu?

5

Over there!

We should help them!

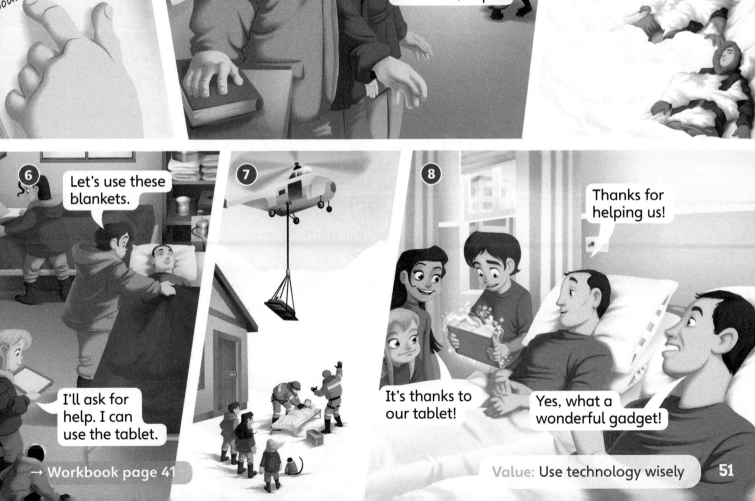

6

Let's use these blankets.

I'll ask for help. I can use the tablet.

7

8

Thanks for helping us!

It's thanks to our tablet!

Yes, what a wonderful gadget!

→ Workbook page 41

Value: Use technology wisely

Skills: *Listening and speaking*

 Let's start! **Which gadgets do you have?**

14 (CD2 26) **What were the first gadgets? Listen and match.**

Adam Osborne   Martin Cooper   Ralph Baer

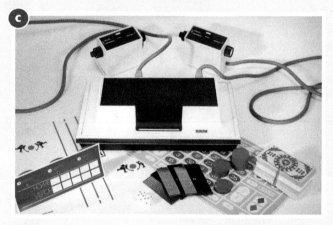

1973   1981   1967–1968

15 (CD2 26) **Listen again and answer the questions.**

1 What was the name of the first games console?
2 How many games were there on the first games console?
3 What was the name of the first laptop?
4 How long was the first cell phone?
5 Where did Martin Cooper get the idea for a cell phone?

16 (CD2 27) (Talk Time) **Decide which inventions are the most useful.**

Which invention is the most useful?   I think it's the ...

What do you use it to do?   I use it to ...

Skills: *Reading and writing*

 What does Max like using his smartphone for?

17 **Read and listen.**

Max is eleven years old, and he likes making movies with his smartphone. We asked him some questions.

How do you make movies?
I think of a story with my friends. Then they act out the story, and I film it.

Where do you make your movies?
We usually go to the park and make the movie outside. Then we go home and edit the movie on my laptop. Editing means choosing the best parts of the movie. I add music and special effects on my laptop, too.

Where do you watch your movies?
On the laptop. Sometimes our parents watch them. They think the movies are funny.

Is making movies difficult?
No. It's easy with a smartphone!

18 **Read again and correct the sentences.**

1 Max is twelve years old.
2 He likes making movies with his digital camera.
3 He makes movies with his cousins.
4 He always makes movies in the park.
5 He edits the movies on a games console.
6 His parents think the movies are boring.

Your turn!

Think of your favorite gadget.
What is it?
What do you like doing with it?

Now write about it in your notebook.

How do we read a line chart?

1 (CD2 29) **Listen and repeat.**

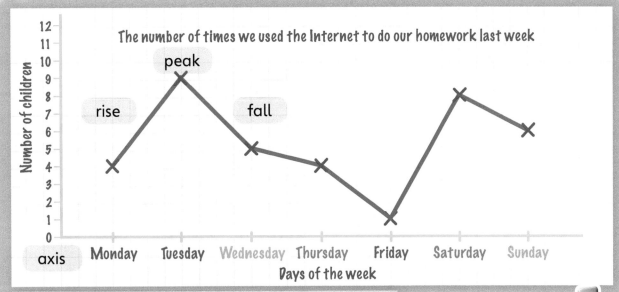

The number of times we used the Internet to do our homework last week

peak

rise

fall

Number of children

axis

Monday Tuesday Wednesday Thursday Friday Saturday Sunday

Days of the week

Mon	Tues	Wed	Thurs	Fri	Sat	Sun
||||	₩₩ ||||	₩|||	||||			₩₩ |||	₩₩	
			data			

Guess What!

Different names for the number 0 include zero, nought, zilch, and zip.

2 **Watch the video.**

3 (CD2 30) **Look at activity 1. Listen and read the data on the line chart.**

4 **Answer the questions.**

1 How many children used the Internet to do their homework on Wednesday?

2 When was there a big rise in the number of children using the Internet?

3 When was there a bigger fall – between Tuesday and Wednesday or between Thursday and Friday?

4 Which day shows the peak number of children using the Internet?

5 **What different data can you put in a line chart?**

Project

6 Find out how often you and your classmates watch television each week. Draw and label a line chart and then put your data into it.

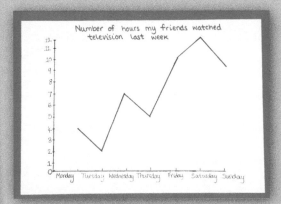

Review Units 3 and 4

 Read, listen, and choose the words.

On my eleventh birthday, I **visit/visited** my favorite **art gallery/movie theater** in London with my family. The movie theater has the **biggest/smallest** screen in the United Kingdom, and it was great.

We watched a very **dangerous/interesting** movie. It was called *Under the Ocean*.

The movie was in 3-D, and we **need/needed** special **headphones/glasses**.

There were lots of beautiful sea animals and some funny ones, too. The **strongest/funniest** one was a crab with a jellyfish on its head! The most **exciting/dangerous** animals were the sea snakes.

We also **listened/learned** about taking care of our oceans.

We should keep them **clean/dirty**.

It was my favorite birthday ever!

Tom

2 **Read again and answer the questions.**
1 How old was Tom?
2 Where did he visit on his birthday?
3 What movie did he watch?
4 What was the funniest sea animal?
5 What did Tom learn about oceans?

3 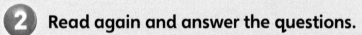 **Think of a visit to the movie theater. Ask and answer.**

What movie did you watch?
Was it in 3-D?
What was it about?

4 **Write about a movie theater visit in your notebook.**

→ Workbook page 46

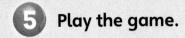

5 Play the game.

TECHNOLOGY FAIR

① **Start**

④ Free headphones! Miss a turn!

③ Watch television/ last night

② Which is the strongest land animal?

⑤ Use an e-reader/ before school

⑦ Visit grand-parents/last weekend

⑥ Which is the most dangerous sea animal?

Which sea animal has eight legs?

Play on the games consoles! Miss a turn!

Which is the most intelligent sea animal?

⑪ Play on a laptop/ yesterday afternoon

⑫ You lose your smartphone. Go back to the start.

⑬ Listen to music/ yesterday evening

⑭ Which dangerous sea animal has a lot of teeth?

⑱ Finish!

⑰ Study English/ last Saturday

⑯ Which is the tallest land animal?

⑮ Watch the digital jellyfish. Miss a turn!

Green
Answer the questions.

Purple
Make true sentences using these words.

57

5 The natural world

Guess What!

1 (CD2 32) **Listen and look.**

2 (CD2 33) **Listen and repeat. Then match.**

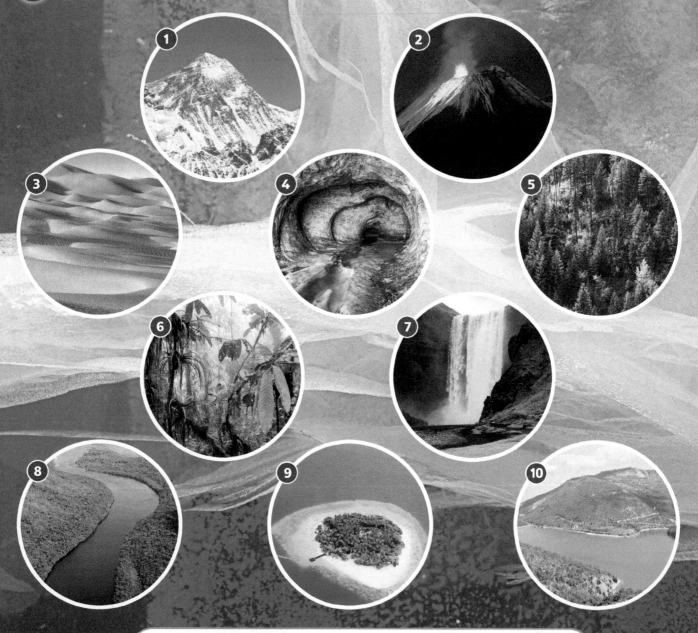

| a cave | b desert | c forest | d island | e jungle |
| f lake | g mountain | h river | i volcano | j waterfall |

3 (CD2 34) (Think) **Listen and say *true* or *false*. Then practice with a friend.**

You can climb a mountain.   True!

4 (My World) **Which of these things would you like to see? Ask and answer.**

5 CD2 35 **Read and listen.**

My family went to Iceland. It was very beautiful. We saw mountains and high waterfalls.

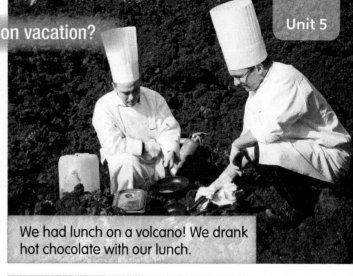

We had lunch on a volcano! We drank hot chocolate with our lunch.

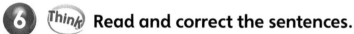

We swam in a lake. The water was warm.

We caught a big fish in a river. Then we ate the fish for dinner. It was delicious.

6 **Read and correct the sentences.**

1 The family went to Russia.
2 They had lunch in a café.
3 They drank orange juice.
4 They swam in a river.
5 They caught a seal in a river.
6 They ate an octopus for dinner.

Focus!

have – had
go – went
see – saw
swim – swam
eat – ate
drink – drank
catch – caught

7 **Think about your vacation last summer. Then ask and answer.**

Where did you go on vacation last summer?
What did you do?
What did you see?
What did you eat and drink?

I went to Baha in Mexico. We swam in the ocean, and we saw whales. We didn't see any sharks.

Say it!

8 CD2 36 CD2 37 **Which words sound the strongest? Listen and repeat.**

We **didn't go** to a **mountain.** We **went** to a **lake**.

→ Workbook page 49   Grammar   Pronunciation   **61**

9 **Where did Emma go on vacation? Listen and choose.**

a a desert **b** a jungle **c** an island

10 **Listen again and practice.**

Alex: Hi, Emma. What are you doing?

Emma: I'm making an album about my vacation. Look, I went to Easter Island.

Alex: Cool! Did you see these statues?

Emma: Yes, I did. They were amazing.

Alex: Did you climb the statues?

Emma: No, I didn't! You shouldn't climb on statues, Alex.

Alex: I know. It was a joke!

> **Focus!**
>
> Did you see statues?
> Yes, I did.
> No, I didn't.

11 (Think) **Think about Alex's vacation scrapbook. Then ask and answer.**

> see animals   swim in a lake   climb a mountain   have a picnic   drink coffee
> go on a boat trip   see a cave   catch a fish   take photographs   visit a museum

Did he see animals?   Yes, he did.

Did he swim in a lake?   No, he didn't.

the mountain we climbed

my sister at our picnic

WHITE SHARK *boat trip*

penguins at the beach

my grandpa and grandma at the market

12 **Go to page 103. Listen and repeat the chant.**

13 CD2 40 Read and listen.

1 Help! I can't see anything. I don't like the dark!

Which country is Hollywood in?

Don't worry, Ruby. We can use the tablet.

2 We're in a cave.

How do we get out?

Let's try this path.

3 Oh, no! I don't like bats!

Don't worry, Sofia.

Let's try the other path.

4 Wow!

Cut!

5 Oh, dear!

We're very sorry!

Don't worry! You can help us.

6 Four actors didn't come this morning.

We're in Hollywood, in the United States!

7 Oh, no! I'm not good at acting.

You're a great actor, Jack!

Action!

8 That was great!

And cut! Thank you, everyone.

→ Workbook page 51

Value: Encourage your friends

Skills: *Listening and speaking*

 Let's start! What is the most interesting animal you can think of?

14 CD2 41 **Where can you find them? Listen and say *rain forest* or *desert*.**

bilby

armadillo lizard

rafflesia

parrot flower

baseball plant

15 CD2 41 **Listen again and choose the words.**

1 Bilbys have long **ears/legs**.
2 Armadillo lizards are **big/small**.
3 The rafflesia is the **oldest/biggest** flower in the world.
4 The parrot flower looks like a **bird/bat**.
5 The baseball plant grows in the **United States/China**.

16 CD2 42 **Talk Time** **Identify animals and plants.**

What's this animal called?   It's called a …

What's this plant called?   It's called a …

Skills: *Reading and writing*

 Look below! **What did Billy do on vacation?**

17 **Read and listen.**

My vacation in the Volcanoes National Park.

We arrived yesterday. The park is very beautiful. There are mountains, volcanoes, and rain forests. There are also about 480 mountain gorillas in the park. We wanted to see them.

You can only visit the gorillas with a guide. We got up very early this morning and walked through the forest for three hours. Then our guide pointed in front of us. We saw a gorilla family!

There was a mother gorilla with a baby and a father gorilla. Father gorillas are called silverbacks, and they're very strong. The gorillas didn't hide – they watched us, too! We stayed close to them for one hour. Then we went back to our hotel. It was the most exciting day of my life!

18 **Read again and answer the questions.**
1 Did Billy go to a desert?
2 How many gorillas live in the park?
3 Did Billy visit the gorillas at night?
4 What are father gorillas called?
5 Were the gorillas interested in Billy?
6 Did he enjoy meeting the gorillas?

Your turn! Think of your favorite vacation.
Where did you go?
What did you do?
What did you see?

Now write about it in your notebook.

What happens when a volcano erupts?

1 CD2 44 Listen and repeat.

| vent | crater | lava | rock | ash |

2 Watch the video.

3 CD2 45 Read and listen.

Volcanoes look like mountains, but volcanoes have a vent inside and a crater at the top. Sometimes they erupt, and very hot, red material comes up the volcano's vent and runs into the crater. This hot material is called lava, and it is very dangerous.

Next, ash and rocks fly high into the air, and the lava runs down the sides of the volcano. After the eruption, the lava gets colder, and it turns to rock.

Lava sometimes runs over plants, and then they stop growing.

A volcano that erupts is called an active volcano. There are about 1,500 active volcanoes in the world.

Guess What!

The world's largest active volcano is Mauna Loa in Hawaii. It is 4,169 m tall.

4 Answer the questions.

1 What does a volcano look like?
2 What is at the top of the volcano?
3 What happens to the very hot, red material when a volcano erupts?
4 How many active volcanoes are there?

5 Which volcano would you like to see?

Project

6 Find out about a volcano in your continent. Write a fact file about it.

Name of volcano: Stromboli
Place: Sicily, Italy
Erupted in: April 2014

6 Helping at home

Guess What!

1 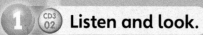 CD3 02 **Listen and look.**

2 CD3 03 **Listen and repeat. Then match.**

a clean the bathroom   b cook dinner   c dry the dishes   d set the table
e make my bed   f take the trash out   g sweep the floor
h clean my bedroom   i wash my clothes   j water the plants

3 CD3 04 Think **Listen and guess the answers. Then practice with a friend.**

What's he doing?   Hmm ... he's taking the trash out!

4 My World **How often do you help at home? Ask and answer.**

5 (CD3 05) **Read and listen. Then read and say the names.**

TUESDAY

Ellen – please clean your room and set the table.

Alfie – please make your bed and water the plants.

Max – please take the trash out and sweep the floor.

Thanks, Mom

1 I have to water the plants, and I have to make my bed. I don't have to take the trash out.

2 My sister has to clean her room, and she has to set the table. She doesn't have to make her bed.

3 My brother doesn't have to clean his room. He has to sweep the floor, and he has to take the trash out.

Focus!

I **have to** make my bed.
I **don't have to** take the trash out.

6 **Read and answer the questions.**

1 Does Ellen have to make her bed?
2 Does Max have to clean his room?
3 Does Alfie have to take the trash out?
4 Does Ellen have to set the table?
5 Does Max have to sweep the floor?

7 (Think) **Write an instruction for a friend. Then mime and guess.**

Please clean the bathroom.

Do you have to clean the bathroom?

Yes, I do.

Say it!

8 (CD3 06) (CD3 07) **Can you hear the different endings? Listen and repeat.**

/s/
plants

/z/
clothes

/iz/
dishes

What does Pedro like doing? Listen and choose.

a collecting the books **b** watering the plants
c feeding the fish

 Listen again and practice.

Alex: What do you have to do today, Pedro?
Pedro: I have to collect the books. What about you?
Alex: I have to water the plants.
Pedro: Who has to feed the fish today?
Alex: Emma does.
Pedro: Lucky her – I love feeding the fish.
Who has to feed the fish tomorrow?
Alex: You do.
Pedro: Oh, good!

  **Look at the classroom schedule.
Then ask and answer.**

Focus!

What do you have to do?
I have to collect the books.
Who has to feed the fish?
Luisa does.

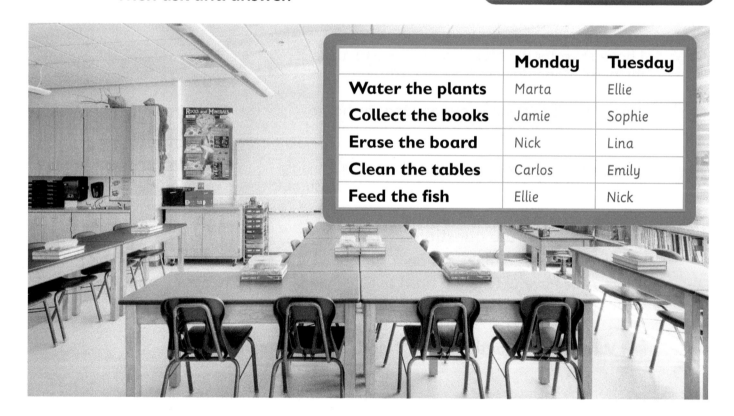

	Monday	Tuesday
Water the plants	Marta	Ellie
Collect the books	Jamie	Sophie
Erase the board	Nick	Lina
Clean the tables	Carlos	Emily
Feed the fish	Ellie	Nick

Who has to erase the board on Monday?

Nick!

What does Nick have to do on Tuesday?

He has to feed the fish.

 Go to page 103. Listen and repeat the chant.

→ Workbook page 58

13 🔊 CD3 10 **Read and listen.**

1. Which river flows through Egypt?

It's a palace in ancient Egypt!

This must be the River Nile.

2. What's wrong?

The king wants to visit today. We have to finish the palace!

We can help.

3.

4. It's beautiful!

Thank you for your help!

5. Look! The King is coming.

6. Oh, no! Where's the key to the palace?

7. Capu! Stop!

No, it's OK. He's a smart monkey!

8. Welcome, King!

It was the key!

Good job, Capu!

Skills: *Listening and speaking*

 Let's start! **What does your home look like?**

14 (CD3 11) **Where do these families live? Listen and say the letters.**

a

b

c

d

15 (CD3 11) **Listen again and say *true* or *false*.**
1 The transparent house is in Japan.
2 The cave house doesn't have a bathroom.
3 The family with the houseboat lives in the United Kingdom.
4 Six giraffes live at the Giraffe Manor hotel.

16 (CD3 12) (Talk Time) **Design your own home.**

It's a cave house. It has …

There are … bedrooms.

The living room is …

The garden has …

Skills: *Reading and writing*

 Look below! What does Sasha do to help at home?

17 **Read and listen.**

Sasha Rudd lives on a farm. What does she have to do at home?

I get up at six o'clock in the morning, and I help with the animals. We have cows, goats, and hens on our farm.

I feed the hens every morning before school. I have to collect the eggs, too. This morning I found six eggs. We had them for breakfast.

On the weekend, I help with the goats. I have to feed them, and I milk them, too. We make cheese with the milk.

I don't have to help with the cows much, but sometimes I have to clean the cowshed after school. That isn't my favorite job!

Life on a farm is hard work, but it's fun. Come and stay!

18 **Read again and say the missing words.**

1 Sasha ▆▆▆▆ ▆▆▆▆ at six o'clock in the morning.
2 There are cows, ▆▆▆▆ , and goats on Sasha's farm.
3 Sasha had eggs for ▆▆▆▆ this morning.
4 Sasha helps with the ▆▆▆▆ on the weekend.
5 Sasha's family makes ▆▆▆▆ with goat's milk.
6 Sasha has to ▆▆▆▆ the cowshed after school.

Your turn!

Think about your day. What do you do before and after school? Do you have to help at home or school?

Now write about it in your notebook.

→ Workbook page 61

What were castle homes like?

1 CD3 14 Listen and repeat.

tower

candle

fire

wall

2 Watch the video.

3 CD3 15 Read and listen.

In the past, some people lived in castles. Most castles had water and big walls around them. The castle walls had tall towers in them. People climbed the towers to see things far away.

Inside the castle there was one very big hall. In this room, families had meals around a long wooden table and talked and listened to music.

Castles had very big kitchens, and people cooked food on open fires. People ate a lot of meat and also bread, fruits, and vegetables. Castles had big gardens, and people grew their own fruits and vegetables. It was very dark at night, and there were no lights. People used candles to see in the dark.

Guess What!

People used wood, not stone, to make the very first castles.

Project

6 Find out about a castle. Make a poster about it.

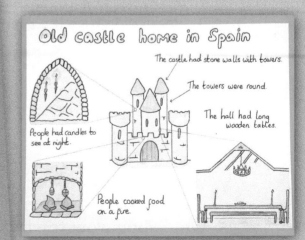

Old castle home in Spain

The castle had stone walls with towers.

The towers were round.

The hall had long wooden tables.

People had candles to see at night.

People cooked food on a fire.

4 Answer the questions.

1 Where did families eat, talk, and listen to music?
2 How did people cook their food?
3 What did people grow in the garden?
4 How did people see in the dark?

5 Would you like to live in an old castle?

Review Units 5 and 6

1  **Read, listen, and choose the words.**

To:

Last month, I went to Loch Ness with my youth club. Loch Ness is a big **island/lake** in **Russia/Scotland**. Some people think a **monster/whale** lives in it. It was an exciting weekend. Some of my friends swam in the lake, but I didn't. The water was very **hot/cold**. We all went on a boat trip, and we looked for the **whale/monster**, but we **saw/didn't see** it.

In the evening, we **went for a walk/ had a picnic** in the **mountains/forest** close to the lake.

Our teacher caught a **fish/monster**, and I had to help cook it for **lunch/ dinner**. Then my friend had to **dry/ wash** the dishes, but we didn't have to set **the table/the bathroom**. We didn't have one!

Becky

2 **Read again and say *true* or *false*.**
1 Becky went to a lake.
2 Becky swam in the lake.
3 Becky didn't see the Loch Ness monster.
4 Becky had to help cook dinner.
5 Her friend had to dry the dishes.

3 **My World** **Think of an exciting trip. Ask and answer.**

Where did you go?
What did you do?
What did you see?

4 **Write about your trip in your notebook.**

→ Workbook page 64

5 Play the game.

7 A _____ is a tropical forest.

7 You don't like spiders! Miss a turn.

6 family? / has / Who / cook / to / dinner / your / in

6 today? / Who / clean / to / has / classroom / the

8 vacation? / volcano / Did / climb / on / a / you

8 sweep / before / Did / school? / you / floor / the

9 An _____ is land with water around it.

5 You have to _____ a messy bedroom.

5 You don't like bats! Miss a turn.

9 You have to _____ plants sometimes.

4 chocolate / Did / drink / hot / you / night? / last

4 eat / octopus / Did / breakfast? / for / you

Good job!

FINISH

3 You have to _____ your bed in the morning.

3 A _____ is a place under the ground.

2 clean / bathroom? / you / have / Do / to / the

ENTER HERE

2 trash? / Do / out / have / you / take / to / the

1 A _____ flows from a mountain to the ocean.

Find the hidden treasure!

1 You have to _____ dirty clothes.

Green
Say the missing words.

Purple
Make a question.

Guess What!

1 CD3 17 **Listen and look.**

2 CD3 18 **Listen and repeat. Then match.**

a angry   **b** bored   **c** excited   **d** hungry   **e** interested
f scared   **g** surprised   **h** thirsty   **i** tired   **j** worried

3 CD3 19 **Listen and say** *true* **or** *false***. Then practice with a friend.**

Look at picture ten. She's scared.   False!

4 My World **Mime a feeling. Ask and answer.**

5 CD3 20 Read, listen, and find. Then say the names.

Focus!

He's scared because he doesn't like spiders.

Jim

Ben   Ali

Emily

Daisy   Lucy

1 He's scared because he doesn't like spiders.
3 They're smiling because they're happy.
5 He's laughing because it's funny.

2 She's eating because she's hungry.
4 He's surprised because there's a spider.

6 Think Read and match.

1 Lucy is happy because …
2 Ben is suprised because …
3 Emily is hungry because …
4 Ali is scared because …
5 It's funny because …

a there's a bird on Jim's head.
b the spider is on his bananas.
c it's breakfast time.
d he really doesn't like spiders.
e she's talking to her friend.

7 My World Make sentences with a friend.

I'm hungry because …   I'm happy because …

Say it!

8 CD3 21 CD3 22 Does the end of the sentence go up or down? Listen and repeat.

I'm surprised because this lesson is easy. ↘   He's laughing because it's funny. ↘

9 Who's scared of sharks? Listen and choose.

a Emma b Emma's sister c Pedro

 10 Listen again and practice.

Pedro: Hi, Emma. How are you today?

Emma: I'm OK, but I'm a little tired.

Pedro: Why are you tired?

Emma: I'm tired because it was my sister's birthday yesterday. We stayed up late and watched a movie.

Pedro: That sounds like fun.

Emma: Yes, but then my sister didn't want to go to bed because she was scared.

Pedro: Why was she scared?

Emma: Because it was a movie about sharks. She's scared of sharks.

Pedro: Oh, no!

Focus!

Why is she tired?
She's tired because she stayed up late.

  11 Read and match. Then ask how your friends are feeling and why.

Why is he thirsty?

Why is she worried?

Why is she excited?

Why is he bored?

Why is she interested?

a Because there isn't any juice. b Because he doesn't like reading.

c Because it's her birthday. d Because she's reading a good book.

e Because the cookies aren't on the plate.

 12 Go to page 103. Listen and repeat the chant.

13 CD3 25 **Read and listen.**

1. Where does the annatto plant grow?

We're in the rain forest in South America.

Why is Capu so excited?

Because this is his home!

2. Ow!

Let's follow Capu!

What's the matter, Jack?

3. It was a snake!

Don't be scared.

We'll help.

4. We need the annatto plant. It grows here.

ANNATTO PLANT

Can you show us, Capu?

5. Can you help us?

Of course. What's the matter?

6. Thank you!

7. Are you OK, Jack?

Yes! They made a medicine with the plant.

8. Goodbye, Capu!

We'll miss you!

→ Workbook page 69

Value: Respect nature   85

Skills: *Listening and speaking*

Let's start! What is your favorite book and why?

14 CD3 26 **What are their favorite books? Listen and match.**

a Goodnight, Mr. Tom, Michelle Magorian

b Horrid Henry, Francesca Simon

Ben   Amber   George   Zoe

c Charlie and the Chocolate Factory, Roald Dahl

d Stay Out of the Basement, R.L. Stine

15 CD3 26 **Listen again and choose the words.**

1 "Stay Out of the Basement" is about two children and their **mother/father/uncle**.
2 The "Horrid Henry" stories are **exciting/funny/sad**.
3 **Four/Five/Six** children visit the factory in "Charlie and the Chocolate Factory."
4 "Goodnight, Mr. Tom" is about a boy and an old **man/woman/horse**.

16 CD3 27 **Talk Time** **Discuss your favorite author.**

Who's your favorite author?

My favorite author is …

What kind of stories does he/she write?

He/She writes …

Skills: *Reading and writing*

 What is Jack climbing?

17 CD3 28 **Read and listen.**

Jack and the Beanstalk

Jack and his mother lived in a village. His mother was often worried because they didn't have any money. One day, Jack had to go to the market and sell their cow. Then he had to buy some food, but Jack only bought five beans.

Jack's mother was very angry. She threw the beans out the window. That night, they grew into a magic beanstalk. Jack and his mother were very surprised.

Jack climbed up the beanstalk. A giant lived in a castle at the top. Jack was scared, but the giant was friendly. He gave Jack a magic hen for his mother. The hen made gold eggs. Jack's mother was very happy, and Jack and the giant were friends.

18 **Read again and answer the questions.**
1 Why was Jack's mother often worried?
2 Where did Jack have to sell the cow?
3 How many beans did Jack buy?
4 Who lived at the top of the beanstalk?
5 Why was the hen magic?
6 How did his mother feel at the end of the story?

Your turn!

Think of a story you know.
Who is in the story?
What happens in the story?
Is the story funny, exciting, sad, or scary?

Now write about it in your notebook.

→ Workbook page 71

How do animals
communicate?

1 (CD3 29) **Listen and repeat.**

growl   flap   hiss   purr   change color

2 **Watch the video.**

3 (CD3 30) **Read and listen.**

Different animals communicate in different ways. Many animals use sounds to communicate with each other. Birds sing, lions, and tigers growl, and turtles can hiss. Chimpanzees touch hands to say "Hello!" Some animals, like frogs and spiders, change color to send messages to each other.

Animals communicate how they feel with their bodies, heads, mouths, and ears. Animals show they are happy in different ways. Polar bears move their heads from side to side, some wild cats purr, and excited elephants flap their ears.

Animals show they are angry in different ways, too. Elephants move very fast, bears growl, and snakes and crocodiles hiss.

Guess What!

Whales jump out of the water to send messages to other whales.

4 **Answer the questions.**

1. How do chimpanzees say "Hello"?
2. How do some frogs and spiders send messages to each other?
3. What body parts do animals use to communicate?
4. How do snakes and crocodiles show they're angry?

5 **How do you communicate your feelings to your family?**

Project

6 **Find out how animals communicate. Make a chart with information about it.**

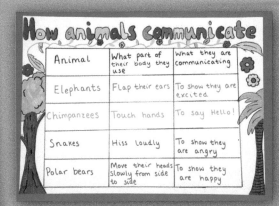

Animal	What part of their body they use	What they are communicating
Elephants	Flap their ears	To show they are excited
Chimpanzees	Touch hands	To say Hello!
Snakes	Hiss loudly	To show they are angry
Polar bears	Move their heads slowly from side to side	To show they are happy

→ Workbook page 72

CLIL: Science **89**

8 Outdoor sports

Guess What!

1 (CD3 31) **Listen and look.**

2 (CD3 32) **Listen and repeat. Then match.**

a bodyboarding   **b** canoeing   **c** go-carting   **d** hiking   **e** rock climbing
f rowing   **g** scuba diving   **h** snorkeling   **i** trampolining   **j** windsurfing

3 (CD3 33) **Listen and answer the questions. Then practice with a friend.**

Look at picture 5. Are they canoeing?

No, they aren't!

4 (My World) **What activities would you like to do? Ask and answer.**

5 (CD3 34) **Read and listen.**

Sam: It was my birthday on Saturday. I went go-carting with my friends. It was really exciting.

Lola: I went trampolining with my friends at the sports center.

Sally: I went to the country with my family. We didn't go hiking. We went canoeing!

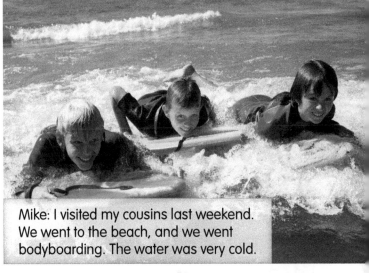

Mike: I visited my cousins last weekend. We went to the beach, and we went bodyboarding. The water was very cold.

Focus!

They **didn't go go-carting** on Saturday.
What **did she do** last weekend?
She **went canoeing.**

6 **Match the questions and answers.**

1 What did Sam do on Saturday?
2 Did Sally go hiking?
3 Did Lola go trampolining?
4 What did Mike do?

a He went bodyboarding.
b Yes, she did.
c He went go-carting.
d No, she didn't.

7 (My World) **Ask and answer.**

What did you do last weekend?   I went hiking.

Did you go windsurfing?   No, I didn't. I went swimming.

8 (CD3 35) **Go to page 103. Listen and repeat the chant.**

What are they talking about? Listen and choose.

a the weekend   b last month   c last year

 Listen again and practice.

Pedro: Can I see your photographs, Carla?
Carla: Yes, of course – it's an album of my year.
Pedro: I like this photograph! Did you go windsurfing last year?
Carla: Yes, I did. I went on an activity vacation with my school.
Pedro: Great! When did you go?
Carla: In March. We went rowing, too.
Pedro: Cool! And when did you go skiing?
Carla: In December.
Pedro: Wow!

Focus!

When **did** you **go** skating?
I **went** skating in December.

  Choose four activities you did last year. Then talk to a friend.

snorkeling   rowing   bodyboarding

sailing   canoeing   swimming   rock climbing

trampolining   windsurfing   ice-skating

fishing   go-carting   hiking   biking

Did you go skiing last year?   Yes, I did.

So did I. When did you go (skiing)?   In February.

Oh! I went in March.

Say it!

 Does the end of the question go up or down? Listen and repeat.

When did you go windsurfing?   What did you do in March?

13 CD3 39 **Read and listen.**

1

Good job, kids.
You finished the quiz.
Now off you fly,
And collect your prize.

Where can we find something to fly?

2

Look! There's a helicopter up there!

Yes, but how do we get there?

3

We can go rock climbing.

OK, but we should be safe. Put on your helmets and follow me.

4

Come on, kids!

Hold on tight to the ropes.

5

It's our town!

And there's the library!

6

Thanks for your help, Sofia.

Do you have to go home?

Yes, I do, but it was fun!

7

Goodbye, Sofia!

See you again soon!

8

Good job! How did you find out the answers?

It's a long story!

PRIZE

→ Workbook page 77

Value: Be safe   95

Skills: *Listening and speaking*

 Let's start! | **What new hobby would you like to try?**

14 (CD3 40) **Which is Malia's club? Listen and choose a picture.**

a

b

15 (CD3 40) **Listen again and say *true* or *false*.**

1 Malia thinks windsurfing is boring.
2 Malia goes to a windsurfing club on Tuesdays.
3 Malia has windsurfing lessons on a lake.
4 Windsurfing can be dangerous.
5 Malia gets scared sometimes.

16 (CD3 41) (Talk Time) **Plan to join a new sports club.**

What sport should we play?   Let's try ...

What equipment do we need?   We need ...

Skills: *Reading and writing*

 Why is this game of volleyball different?

17 (CD3 42) **Read and listen.**

Let's try something different!

Do you like trampolining? Try bossaball! Bossaball is like volleyball, but you play on a trampoline. There are two teams. The players hit or kick the ball over a net. The ball hits the floor, and the team gets a point.

Can you swim underwater? What about playing hockey? Underwater hockey started in the United Kingdom. Now people play it all over the world. There are two teams. The players have to push a hockey puck at the bottom of a pool. It's also called "Octopush."

Do you enjoy body boarding? Do you have a dog? How about a dog surfing competition? Dog surfing competitions are popular in California, in the United States. There are competitions every year.

18 **Read again and say the missing words.**
1 Bossaball is like   .
2 You play bossaball on a   .
3 You play underwater   in a swimming pool.
4 There are   teams in underwater hockey.
5   surfing is popular in the United States.
6 There are competitions every   .

Your turn! **Think of an unusual sport.** Where do you play it? How do you play?

Now write about it in your notebook.

What makes our bodies move?

1 🎵 CD3 43 Listen and repeat.

bone   muscle   knee   elbow   joint

2 Watch the video.

3 🎵 CD3 44 Read and listen.

We move our bodies a lot for sports because we run, jump, bend, and stretch. We use our bones, muscles, and joints.

Two or more bones meet at our joints. Elbows are joints in our arms, and knees are joints in our legs. We have lots of muscles in our body, from our faces to our feet. Muscles are connected to our bones. Muscles get longer or shorter to make our joints and bones move.

We need strong bones, muscles, and joints for sports. Some sports, like hiking, use our leg muscles. Some sports, like rowing, use our arm muscles. Some sports, like rock climbing, use leg, arm, and other muscles in our body.

Guess What!

We use 17 muscles in our face to smile and 43 muscles to frown!

Project

6 Choose three sports you enjoy. Make a leaflet showing the parts of the body you use for each sport.

4 Answer the questions.

1 What do we use to move our bodies?
2 Where are our knee and elbow joints?
3 How do our muscles help us move?
4 Why should our bones, muscles, and joints be strong?

5 Which parts of your body are the strongest and the weakest?

Review Units 7 and 8

1 CD3 45 **Read, listen, and choose the words.**

My scariest experience was last year. I was on vacation with my parents, and we went **rock climbing/hiking** in the mountains.

I was a little **bored/excited** at first. I like **hiking/rock climbing**, but we **climbed/walked** for a long time, and we didn't see anything.

Then suddenly we saw a brown **gorilla/bear**. It was really **close to/far away** from us, but I was very **excited/scared**.

We were lucky **because/but** the **gorilla/bear** didn't see us. We turned around and **walked/ran** away. We didn't **shout/laugh** or **skip/run**.

The people at the hotel were **interested in/ surprised by** our story, but after that I didn't want to go into the mountains again. I went **rowing/ trampolining** instead.

Josh

2 **Read again and answer the questions.**

1   Why was Josh bored?
2   Was the animal close to them?
3   Was Josh scared?
4   Did his family run away?
5   Why did Josh go trampolining the next day?

3 My World **Think of your scariest experience. Ask and answer.**

When did it happen?
What happened?
How did you feel?

4 **Write about your scariest experience in your notebook.**

→ Workbook page 82

5 Play the game.

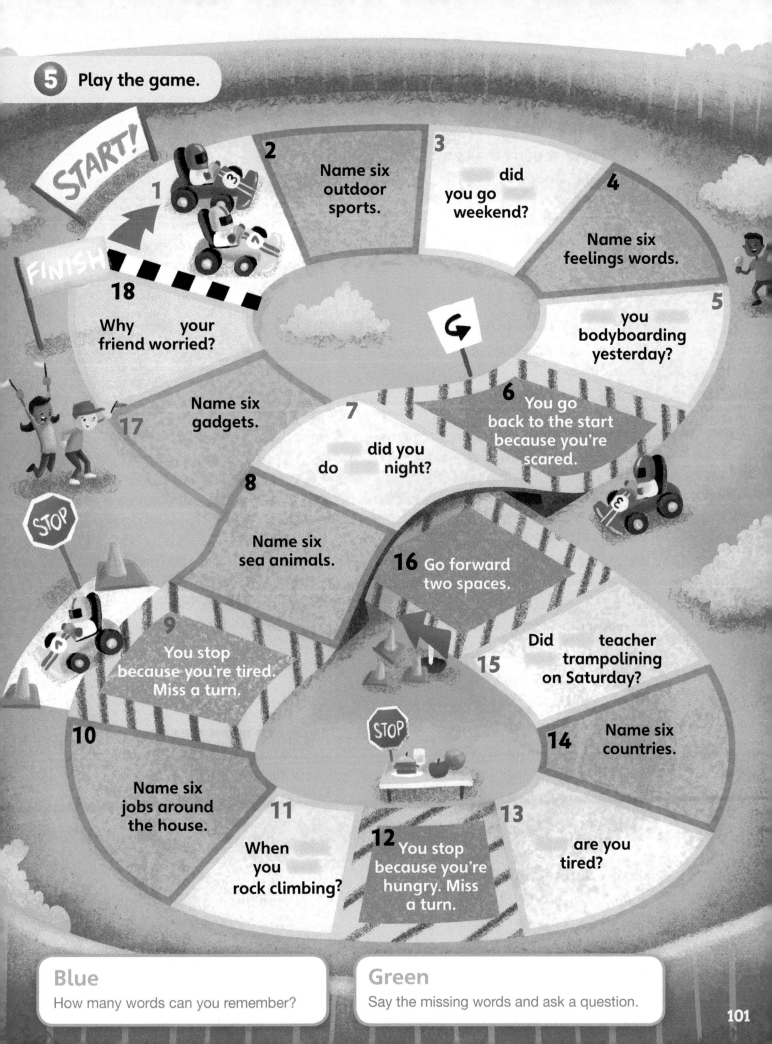

START!

FINISH

1

2 Name six outdoor sports.

3 _____ did you go _____ weekend?

4 Name six feelings words.

5 _____ you bodyboarding yesterday?

6 You go back to the start because you're scared.

7 _____ do _____ did you _____ night?

8 Name six sea animals.

9 You stop because you're tired. Miss a turn.

10 Name six jobs around the house.

11 When _____ you rock climbing?

12 You stop because you're hungry. Miss a turn.

13 _____ are you tired?

14 Name six countries.

15 Did _____ teacher _____ trampolining on Saturday?

16 Go forward two spaces.

17 Name six gadgets.

18 Why _____ your friend worried?

STOP

STOP

Blue
How many words can you remember?

Green
Say the missing words and ask a question.

101

Chants

Welcome (page 7)

 Listen and repeat the chant.

Where are you from?
I'm from Russia.
Are you from Russia?
No, I'm not. I'm from Spain.

Where is he from?
He's from Russia.
Is she from Russia?
No, she isn't. She's from Spain.

Unit 1 (page 17)

 Listen and repeat the chant.

Are you shyer than your sister?
Yes, I am.
She's more talkative than me.
Are you smarter than your sister?
No, I'm not.
She's smarter than me.

Is your friend sportier than you?
No, he isn't.
I'm sportier than him.
Is your friend naughtier than you?
Yes, he's naughtier than me,
My friend's as naughty as can be!

Unit 2 (page 27)

 Listen and repeat the chant.

We should be polite and hardworking.
We shouldn't be naughty in school!
We shouldn't laugh at others.
We should be good in school!

We should listen to our teachers.
We shouldn't be naughty in school!
We shouldn't shout in the classroom.
We should be good in school!

Unit 3 (page 40)

 Listen and repeat the chant.

Which fish is the biggest?
The biggest fish, the biggest fish?
Which fish is the biggest?
I think it's a whale shark!

Which bird is the strongest?
The strongest bird, the strongest bird?
Which bird is the strongest?
I think it's the eagle!

Unit 4 (page 49)

 Listen and repeat the chant.

I didn't watch TV last night.
I played a computer game.
I used my laptop last night.
She played a computer game.

I didn't play on my tablet.
I studied for a test.
I used my new e-reader.
He studied for a test.

Unit 5 (page 62)

 Listen and repeat the chant.

Did you have a
nice time
On your vacation?
Yes, we did – a very
nice time
On our vacation.

Did you go on a
boat trip
On your vacation?
No, we didn't – we
swam in a lake
On our vacation.

Did you go on a picnic
On your vacation?
Yes, we did – we
ate too much
On our vacation!

Unit 6 (page 72)

 Listen and repeat the chant.

Who has to collect the books?
Max does, Max does.
Who has to water the plants?
Kim does, Kim does.

Who has to feed the fish?
You do, you do!
I do? OK.
I'll feed the fish today.

Unit 7 (page 84)

 Listen and repeat the chant.

Why are you tired today?
Why are you tired?
I'm tired because I stayed up late.
And now I'm very tired.

Why are you worried today?
Why are you worried?
I'm worried because the test is today.
And now I'm very worried.

Unit 8 (page 93)

 Listen and repeat the chant.

Where did you go on the weekend?
I went to the beach with my friends.
We didn't go swimming or snorkeling.
We went bodyboarding instead.

Where did he go on the weekend?
He went to the beach with his friends.
They didn't go swimming or snorkeling.
They went bodyboarding instead.

Thanks and Acknowledgments

Many thanks to everyone in the excellent team at Cambridge University Press. In particular we would like to thank Emily Hird, Liane Grainger, and Melissa Bryant whose professionalism, enthusiasm, experience, and talent makes them all such a pleasure to work with.

We would also like to give special thanks to Lesley Koustaff for her unfailing support, expert guidance, good humor, and welcome encouragement throughout the project.

The authors and publishers would like to thank the following contributors:

Blooberry Design: concept design, cover design, book design, page makeup
Bridget Kelly: editing
Ann Thomson: art direction, picture research
Gareth Boden Photography: commissioned photography
Alison Wright: picture research
Lisa Hutchins: freelance editing
Ian Harker: audio recording
Robert Lee, Dib Dib Dub Studios: chant composition
James Richardson: arrangement of theme tune
John Marshall Media: audio recording and production
Vince Cross: theme tune composition
Phaebus: video production
hyphen S.A.: publishing management, American English edition

The authors and publishers acknowledge the following sources of copyright material and are grateful for the permissions granted. Although every effort has been made, it has not always been possible to identify the sources of all the material used, or to trace all copyright holders. If any omissions are brought to our notice, we will be happy to include the appropriate acknowledgments on reprinting.

The authors and publishers would like to thank the following illustrators:

Pablo Gallego (Beehive Illustration): pp. 9, 19, 29, 41, 51, 63, 73, 85, 95; Mark Duffin p. 32; Marcus Cutler (Sylvie Poggio): pp. 35, 57, 79, 101; Graham Kennedy: p. 87.

The authors and publishers would like to thank the following for permission to reproduce photographs:

Chants spread b/g: Shutterstock; Contents b/g: Eduardo Gonzalez Diaz/Alamy; p. 4-5: Tim Gainey/Alamy; p. 6 (map b/g): Getty/Image Source; p. 6 (flag 1): Shutterstock/Charnsit Ramyarupa: p. 6 (flag 2): Bob Petit/MapQuest/Shutterstock; p. 6 (flag 3): Paul Stringer/Shutterstock; p. 6 (flag 4): Bob Petit/MapQuest/Shutterstock; p. 6 (flag 5): Shutterstock; p. 6 (flag 6): Shutterstock; p. 6 (flag 7): Shutterstock; p. 6 (flag 8): zzns/Shutterstock; p. 6 (flag 9): Bob Petit/MapQuest/Shutterstock; p. 6 (flag 10): Bob Petit/MapQuest/Shutterstock; p. 7 (TL): Tanya Ustenko/Shutterstock; p. 7 (TR): Cultura Creative/Alamy; p. 7 (BL): Radius Images/Alamy; p. 7 (BR): RimDream/Shutterstock; p. 10 (1): Christine Whitehead/Alamy; p. 10 (2): SandiMako/Shutterstock; p. 10 (3): Peter Adams/Getty; p. 10 (4): ANDRE DURAO/Shutterstock; p. 10 (5): Blend Images/Alamy; p. 11 (girl): Norman Price/Alamy; p. 11 (sculpture): Ekaterina Bykova/Shutterstock; p. 12: John Dunne/Getty; p. 13 (1): marekuliasz/Shutterstock; p. 13 (2): Destinyweddingstudio/Shutterstock; p. 13 (3): dbimages/Alamy; p. 13 (4): BRYANT Nicolas/SAGAPHOTO.COM/Alamy; p. 13 (BR): Sergei Aleshin/Shutterstock; p. 14-15: Wilfried Martin/Getty; p. 16 (b/g): elenaleonova/Getty; p. 16 (1): Menzl Guenter/Shutterstock; p. 16 (2): Amir Kaljikovic/Shutterstock; p. 16 (3): VStock LLC/Tanya Constantine/Getty; p. 16 (4): Ian Allenden/Alamy; p. 16 (5): ZouZou/Shutterstock; p. 16 (6): Przemek Klos/Shutterstock; p. 16 (7): Shots Studio/Shutterstock; p. 16 (8): WEExp/Shutterstock; p. 16 (9): Vasilyev Alexandr/Shutterstock; p. 16 (10): Anneka/Shutterstock; p. 20 (b/g): Marcus LindstrAm/Getty; p. 20 (TL): Q-Images/Alamy; p. 20 (TR): Nick Turner/Alamy; p. 20 (BL): imageBROKER/Alamy; p. 20 (BR): epa european pressphoto agency b.v./Alamy; p. 21 (T): Tom Stewart/Corbis; p. 21 (BL): Fuse/Getty; p. 21 (BR): elic/Shutterstock; p. 22-23: TeguhSantosa/Getty; p. 23 (1): noolwlee/Shutterstock; p. 23 (2): Johner Images/Corbis; p. 23 (3): pattara puttiwong/Shutterstock; p. 23 (4): Alex Wild/Corbis; p. 23 (5): National Geographic Image Collection/Alamy; p. 24-25: J. McPhail/Shutterstock; p. 26 (b/g): Giorgio Fochesato/Getty; p. 26 (1): Purestock/Alamy; p. 26 (2): altrendo images/Getty; p. 26 (3): Alistair Berg/Getty; p. 26 (4): KidStock/Getty; p. 26 (5): Rob Friedman/Getty; p. 26 (6): 2/Ocean/Corbis; p. 26 (7): iofoto/Shutterstock; p. 26 (8): MJTH/Shutterstock; p. 26 (9): Peter Alvey/Alamy; p. 28 (10): Cultura Creative/Alamy; p. 27 (b/g): Tom Wang/Shutterstock; p. 30-31 (b/g): clubfoto/Getty; p. 31 (1): Werli Francois/Alamy; p. 31 (a): Jon Bower UK/

Alamy; p. 31 (2): syaochka/Shutterstock; p. 31 (b): David Bathgate/Corbis; p. 32 (CLIL b/g): Sergey Borisov/Alamy; p. 33 (T): billy bonns/Shutterstock; p. 34: LWA/Dann Tardif/Getty; p. 36-37: Michael Moxter/Getty; p. 38 (b/g): Ulrike Neumann/Getty; p. 38 (1): Steve Noakes/Shutterstock; p. 38 (2): Kevin Schafer/Alamy; p. 38 (3): Photos by Carol/Getty; p. 38 (4): Tim Fitzharris/Getty; p. 38 (5): Panoramic Images/Getty; p. 38 (6): Stefan Pircher/Shutterstock; p. 38 (7): Reinhard Dirscherl/Getty; p. 38 (8): imageBROKER/Alamy; p. 38 (9): Jocelyn Winwood, NZ/Getty; p. 38 (10): Nature Picture Library/Alamy; p. 39 (TL): Christian Musat/Alamy; p. 39 (TR): MR1805/Getty; p. 39 (BL): joebelanger/Getty; p. 39 (BR): Paul Sutherland/Getty; p. 40 (B): Darran Rees/Corbis; p. 42 (a): Nature/UIG/Getty; p. 42 (b): kali9/Getty; p. 42 (c); Daniela Stolfi/Getty; p. 42 (d): Photos by Carol/Getty; p. 42 (e): Yulia Popkova/Getty; p. 43: Csondy/Getty; p. 44: Zac Macaulay/Corbis; p. 45 (1): Stefan Deutsch/Corbis; p. 45 (2): Carlos Villoch - MagicSea.com/Alamy; p. 45 (3): Artem Rudik/Shutterstock; p. 45 (4); Carlos Villoch - MagicSea.com/Alamy; p. 46-47; Scott Stulberg/Corbis; p. 48 (b/g): Brian Stablyk/Getty; p. 48 (1): FERNANDO BLANCO CALZADA/Shutterstock; p. 48 (2): Jiri Hera/Shutterstock; p. 48 (3): K. Miri Photography/Shutterstock; p. 48 (4): keellla/Shutterstock; p. 48 (5): Valentina Razumova/Shutterstock; p. 48 (6): neelsky/Shutterstock; p. 48 (7): Maxx-Studio/Shutterstock; p. 48 (8): p.48 (8 screen): Tara Farquhar/EyeEm/GettyRF; Oleg GawriloFF/Shutterstock; p. 48 (9): Igor Lateci/Shutterstock; p. 48 (9 screen): Deb Casso/Getty; p. 48 (10): Julien_N/Shutterstock; p. 49 (TL): Britta Pedersen/Corbis; p. 49 (TR): Blend Images/Alamy; p. 49 (BL): Meibion/Alamy; p. 49 (BR): Goodluz/Shutterstock; p. 50 (B): Multi-bits/Getty; p. 52 (1): INTERFOTO/Alamy; p. 52 (2): Bloomberg/Getty; p. 52 (3): Magnavox Corporation/Science and Society Photo Library; p. 54: All Canada Photos/Alamy; p. 56: Ale Ventura/Corbis; p. 58-59: George Steinmetz/Corbis; p. 60 (b/g): Cultura RM/Seb Oliver/Getty; p. 60 (1): Galyna Andrushko/Shutterstock; p. 60 (2): Pablo Hidalgo - Fotos593/Shutterstock; p. 60 (3): Andrea Willmore/Shutterstock; p. 60 (4): Filip Fuxa/Shutterstock; p. 60 (5): Chris Gardiner/Shutterstock; p. 60 (6): Dr. Morley Read/Shutterstock; p. 60 (7): lenaer/Shutterstock; p. 60 (8): Janne Hamalainen/Shutterstock; p. 60 (9): VVO/Shutterstock; p. 60 (10): Drimi/Shutterstock; p. 61 (TL): javarman/Shutterstock; p. 61 (TR): Kristjan Logason/Demotix/Corbis; p. 61 (BL): Robert Hoetink/Shutterstock; p. 61 (BR): holbox/Shutterstock; p. 62 (L): orangecrush/Shutterstock; p. 62 (M): Eugene Sergeev/Alamy; p. 62 (TR): Four Oaks/Shutterstock; p. 62 (BR): Eric Nathan/Alamy; p. 64 (TL): Martin Harvey/Alamy; p. 64 (TR): M-Net Local Productions/Getty; p. 64 (BL): kkaplin/Shutterstock; p. 64 (BM): WhyMePhoto/Shutterstock; p. 64 (BR): Florapix/Alamy; p. 65 (b/g): Rolf Nussbaumer Photography/Alamy; p. 65 (T): Image Source/Alamy; p. 66: Getty; p. 67 (1): Greg Vaughn/Getty; p. 67 (2): O. Louis Mazzatenta/Getty; p. 67 (3): Nordroden/Shutterstock; p. 67 (4): Tamara Kulikova/Shutterstock; p. 67 (5): wdeon/Shutterstock; p. 67 (6): luigi nifosi/Shutterstock; p. 68-69: Jupiterimages/Getty; p. 70 (b/g): WLADIMIR BULGAR/Getty; p. 70 (1): John Birdsall/Rex; p. 70 (2): Blend Images/Alamy; p. 70 (3): Arina P Habich/Shutterstock; p. 70 (4): Blend Images/Shutterstock; p. 70 (5): MBI/Alamy; p. 70 (6): Jupiterimages/Getty; p. 70 (7): Shotshop GmbH/Alamy; p. 70 (8): Alamy; p. 70 (9): Barry Austin Photography/Getty; p. 70 (10): tmcphotos/Shutterstock; p. 71 (TL): Monkey Business Images/Shutterstock; p. 70 (TR): vario images GmbH & Co.KG/Alamy; p. 72 (B): Sam Kittner/kittner.com/Getty; p. 74 (a): The Photolibrary Wales/Alamy; p. 74 (b): Frans Lanting/Corbis; p. 74 (c): Aflo Co. Ltd./Alamy; p. 74 (d): Lukasz Janyst/Shutterstock; p. 75: John Coletti/Getty; p. 76: Weyers, L./Corbis; p. 76 (1): Andrey Starostin/Shutterstock; p. 76 (2): Aksenova Natalya/Shutterstock; p. 76 (3): Kletr/Shutterstock; p. 76 (4): Rob Swanson/Shutterstock; p. 78: Bucchi Francesco/Shutterstock; p. 80-81: Chad Slattery/Getty; p. 82 (b/g): Peter Dazeley/Getty; p. 83 (TL): blickwinkel/Alamy; p. 83 (BL): PathDoc/Alamy; p. 86 (b/g): Thinglass/Shutterstock; p. 86 (main): KidStock/Getty; p. 88: Randy Wells/Corbis; p. 89 (1): Scott E Read/Shutterstock; p. 89 (2): Martin Harvey/Alamy; p. 89 (3): Maria Dryfhout/Corbis; p. 89 (4): Muythaisong Pitakpong/Shutterstock; p. 89 (5): I love nature/Getty; p. 90-91: mountainberryphoto/Getty; p. 92 (b/g): Dimitar Kunev/Shutterstock; p. 92 (1): Pierre Jacques/Corbis; p. 92 (2): Cultura Creative/Alamy; p. 92 (3): stephen brian/Alamy; p. 92 (4): Robin Weaver/Alamy; p. 92 (5): imageBROKER/Alamy; p. 92 (6): Catchlight Visual Services/Alamy; p. 92 (7): BlueOrange Studio/Shutterstock; p. 92 (8): Arterra Picture Library/Alamy; p. 92 (9): Max Topchii/Shutterstock; p. 92 (10): Charles Hood/Alamy; p. 93 (TL): ALAN OLIVER/Alamy; p. 93 (TR): Blend Images/Alamy; p. 93 (BL): Brocreative/Shutterstock; p. 93 (BR): Radius Images/Alamy; p. 94 (B): Michael DeYoung/Corbis; p. 96 (L): Patryk Kosmider/Shutterstock; p. 96 (R): Matyas Rehak/Shutterstock; p. 97: RODRIGO OROPEZA/Corbis; p. 98: John P Kelly/Getty; p. 99 (1): Sebastian Kaulitzki/Shutterstock; p. 99 (2): Alamy; p. 99 (3): Image Source/Alamy; p. 99 (4): Image Source/Alamy; p. 99 (5): BlueRing_Boumy/Shutterstock; p. 100: All Canada Photos/Alamy.

Commissioned photography by Gareth Boden: p. 8 (TR), (B); p. 13 (BR); p. 17; p. 18; p. 23 (BR), p. 28; p. 30; p. 33 (BR); p. 40 (TR); p. 45 (BR); p. 50 (TR); pp. 53-54 (B/G); p. 55 (BR); p. 62 (TR); p. 67 (BR); p. 72 (TR); p. 77 (BR); p. 82; p.83 (TR, BR); p. 84; p.89 (BR); p.94 (TR); p. 99 (BR).

Our special thanks to the following for their kind help during location photography:

Coleridge Community College, Parkside Federation Academies

Front Cover photo by aghezzi/Getty Images